Python Machine learning

Beginner's guide to get you started with Machine

learning and Deep learning with Python

TABLE OF CONTENTS

This document is geared towards providing exact and reliable information in regards to the topic and issue covered. The publication is sold with the idea that the publisher is not required to render accounting, officially permitted, or otherwise, qualified services. If advice is necessary, legal or professional, a practiced individual in the profession should be ordered.

- From a Declaration of Principles which was accepted and approved equally by a Committee of the American Bar Association and a Committee of Publishers and Associations.

The information provided herein is stated to be truthful and consistent, in that any liability, in terms of inattention or otherwise, by any usage or abuse of any policies, processes, or directions contained within is the solitary and utter responsibility of the recipient reader. Under no circumstances will any legal responsibility or blame be held against the publisher for any reparation, damages, or monetary loss due to the information herein, either directly or indirectly.

Respective authors own all copyrights not held by the publisher.

The information herein is offered for informational purposes solely, and is universal as so. The presentation of the information is without contract or any type of guarantee assurance.

The trademarks that are used are without any consent, and the publication of the trademark is without permission or backing by the trademark owner. All trademarks and brands within this book are for clarifying purposes only and are the owned by the owners themselves, not affiliated with this document.

PREFACE

I probably don't need to tell you that machine learning has become one of the most exciting technologies of our time and age. Big companies, such as Google, Facebook, Apple, Amazon, IBM, and many more, heavily invest in machine learning research and applications for good reasons. Although it may seem that machine learning has become the buzzword of our time and age, it is certainly not a hype. This exciting field opens the way to new possibilities and has become indispensable to our daily lives. Talking to the voice assistant on our smart phones, recommending the right product for our customers, stopping credit card fraud, filtering out spam from our e-mail inboxes, detecting and diagnosing medical diseases, the list goes on and on.

If you want to become a machine learning practitioner, a better problem solver, or maybe even consider a career in machine learning research, then this book is for you! However, for a novice, the theoretical concepts behind machine learning can be quite overwhelming. Yet, many practical books that have been published in recent years will help you get started in machine learning by implementing powerful learning algorithms. In my opinion, the use of practical code examples serve an important purpose.

They illustrate the concepts by putting the learned material directly into action. However, remember that with great power comes great responsibility! The concepts behind machine learning are too beautiful and important to be hidden in a black box. Thus, my personal mission is to provide you with a different book; a book that discusses the necessary details regarding machine learning concepts, offers intuitive yet informative explanations on how machine learning algorithms work, how to use them, and most importantly, how to avoid the most common pitfalls.

If you type "machine learning" as a search term in Google Scholar, it returns an overwhelmingly large number-1,800,000 publications. Of course, we cannot discuss all the nitty-gritty details about all the different algorithms and applications that have emerged in the last 60 years. However, in this book, we will embark on an exciting journey that covers all the essential topics and concepts to give you a head start in this field. If you find that your thirst for knowledge is not satisfied, there are many useful resources that can be used to follow up on the essential breakthroughs in this field.

If you have already studied machine learning theory in detail, this book will show you how to put your knowledge into practice. If you have used machine learning techniques before and want to gain more insight into how machine learning really works, this book is for you! Don't worry if you are completely new to the machine learning field; you have even more reason to be excited. I promise you that machine learning will change the way you think about the problems you want to solve and will show you how to tackle them by unlocking the power of data.

Before we dive deeper into the machine learning field, let me answer your most important question, "why Python?" The answer is simple: it is powerful yet very accessible. Python has become the most popular programming language for data science because it allows us to forget about the tedious parts of programming and offers us an environment where we can quickly jot down our ideas and put concepts directly into action.

Reflecting on my personal journey, I can truly say that the study of machine learning made me a better scientist, thinker, and problem solver. In this book, I want to share this knowledge with you. Knowledge is gained by learning, the key is our enthusiasm, and the true mastery of skills can only be achieved by practice. The road ahead may be bumpy on occasions, and some topics may be more challenging than others, but I hope that you will embrace this opportunity and focus on the reward.

Remember that we are on this journey together, and throughout this book, we will add many powerful techniques to your arsenal that will help us solve even the toughest problems the data-driven way.

Introduction

Data is the new oil and Machine Learning is a powerful concept and framework for making the best out of it. In this age of automation and intelligent systems, it is hardly a surprise that Machine Learning and Data Science are some of the top buzz words. The tremendous interest and renewed investments in the field of Data Science across industries, enterprises, and domains are clear indicators of its enormous potential. Intelligent systems and data-driven organizations are becoming a reality and the advancements in tools and techniques is only helping it expand further. With data being of paramount importance, there has never been a higher demand for Machine Learning and Data Science practitioners than there is now. Indeed, the world is facing a shortage of data scientists. It's been coined "The sexiest job in the 21st Century" which makes it all the more worthwhile to try to build some valuable expertise in this domain.

Practical Machine Learning with Python is a problem solver's guide to building real-world intelligent systems. It follows a comprehensive three-tiered approach packed with concepts, methodologies, hands-on examples, and code. This book helps its readers master the essential skills needed to recognize and solve complex problems with Machine Learning and Deep Learning by following a data-driven mindset. Using real-world case studies that leverage the popular Python Machine Learning ecosystem, this book is your perfect companion for learning the art and science of Machine Learning to become a successful practitioner.

The concepts, techniques, tools, frameworks, and methodologies used in this book will teach you how to think, design, build, and execute Machine Learning systems and projects successfully.

This book will get you started on the ways to leverage the Python Machine Learning ecosystem with its diverse set of frameworks and libraries. The three-tiered approach of this book starts by focusing on building a strong foundation around the basics of Machine Learning and relevant tools and frameworks, the next part emphasizes the core processes around building Machine Learning pipelines, and the final part leverages this knowledge on solving some real-world case studies from diverse domains, including retail, transportation, movies, music, computer vision, art, and finance. We also cover a wide range of Machine Learning models, including regression, classification, forecasting, rule-mining, and clustering. This book also touches on cutting edge methodologies and research from the field of Deep Learning, including concepts like transfer learning and case studies relevant to computer vision, including image classification and neural style transfer.

The main intent of this book is to give a wide range of readers — including IT professionals, analysts, developers, data scientists, engineers, and graduate students — a structured approach to gaining essential skills pertaining to Machine Learning and enough knowledge about leveraging state-of-the-art Machine Learning techniques and frameworks so that they can start solving their own real-world problems.

This book is application-focused, so it's not a replacement for gaining deep conceptual and theoretical knowledge about Machine Learning algorithms, methods, and their internal implementations. We strongly recommend you supplement the practical knowledge gained through this book with some standard books on data mining, statistical analysis, and theoretical aspects of Machine Learning algorithms and methods to gain deeper insights into the world of Machine Learning.

CHAPTER ONE

Machine Learning Basics

The idea of making intelligent, sentient, and self-aware machines is not something that suddenly came into existence in the last few years. In fact a lot of lore from Greek mythology talks about intelligent machines and inventions having self-awareness and intelligence of their own. The origins and the evolution of the computer have been really revolutionary over a period of several centuries, starting from the basic Abacus and its descendant the slide rule in the 17th Century to the first general purpose computer designed by Charles Babbage in the 1800s. In fact, once computers started evolving with the invention of the Analytical Engine by Babbage and the first computer program, which was written by Ada Lovelace in 1842, people started wondering and contemplating that could there be a time when computers or machines truly become intelligent and start thinking for themselves. In fact, the renowned computer scientist, Alan Turing, was highly influential in the development of theoretical computer science, algorithms, and formal language and addressed concepts like artificial intelligence and Machine Learning as early as the 1950s. This brief insight into the evolution of making machines learn is just to give you an idea of something that has been out there since centuries but has recently started gaining a lot of attention and focus.

With faster computers, better processing, better computation power, and more storage, we have been living in what I like to call, the "age of information" or the "age of data". Day in and day out, we deal with managing Big Data and building intelligent systems by using concepts and methodologies from Data Science, Artificial Intelligence, Data Mining, and Machine Learning. Of course, most of you must have heard many of the terms I just mentioned and come across sayings like "data is the new oil". The main challenge that businesses and organizations have embarked on in the last decade is to use approaches to try to make sense of all the data that they have and use valuable information and insights from it in order to make better decisions. Indeed with great advancements in technology, including availability of cheap and massive computing, hardware (including GPUs) and storage, we have seen a thriving ecosystem built around domains like Artificial Intelligence, Machine Learning, and most recently Deep Learning. Researchers, developers, data scientists, and engineers are working continuously round the clock to research and build tools, frameworks, algorithms, techniques, and methodologies to build intelligent models and systems that can predict events, automate tasks, perform complex analyses, detect anomalies, self-heal failures, and even understand and respond to human inputs.

This chapter follows a structured approach to cover various concepts, methodologies, and ideas associated with Machine Learning. The core idea is to give you enough background on why we need Machine Learning, the fundamental building blocks of Machine Learning, and what Machine Learning offers us presently. This will enable you to learn about how best you can leverage Machine Learning to get the maximum from your data. Since this is a book on practical Machine Learning, while we will be focused on specific use cases, problems, and real-world case studies in subsequent chapters, it is extremely important to understand formal definitions, concepts, and foundations with regard to learning algorithms, data management, model building, evaluation, and deployment. Hence, we cover all these aspects, including industry standards related to data mining and Machine Learning workflows, so that it gives you a foundational framework that can be applied to approach and tackle any of the real-world problems we solve in subsequent chapters. Besides this, we also cover the different inter-disciplinary fields associated with Machine Learning, which are in fact related fields all under the umbrella of artificial intelligence.

The Need for Machine Learning

Human beings are perhaps the most advanced and intelligent lifeform on this planet at the moment. We can think, reason, build, evaluate, and solve complex problems. The human brain is still something we ourselves haven't figured out completely and hence artificial intelligence is still something that's not surpassed human intelligence in several aspects. Thus you might get a pressing question in mind as to why do we really need Machine Learning? What is the need to go out of our way to spend time and effort to make machines learn and be intelligent? The answer can be summed up in a simple sentence, "To make data-driven decisions at scale". We will dive into details to explain this sentence in the following sections.

Making Data-Driven Decisions

Getting key information or insights from data is the key reason businesses and organizations invest heavily in a good workforce as well as newer paradigms and domains like Machine Learning and artificial intelligence. The idea of data-driven decisions is not new. Fields like operations research, statistics, and management information systems have existed for decades and attempt to bring efficiency to any business or organization by using data and analytics to make data-driven decisions. The art and science of leveraging your data to get actionable insights and make better decisions is known as making data-driven decisions.

Of course, this is easier said than done because rarely can we directly use raw data to make any insightful decisions. Another important aspect of this problem is that often we use the power of reasoning or intuition to try to make decisions based on what we have learned over a period of time and on the job. Our brain is an extremely powerful device that helps us do so. Consider problems like understanding what your fellow colleagues or friends are speaking, recognizing people in images, deciding whether to approve or reject a business transaction, and so on. While we can solve these problems almost involuntary, can you explain someone the process of how you solved each of these problems? Maybe to some extent, but after a while, it would be like, "Hey! My brain did most of the thinking for me!" This is exactly why it is difficult to make machines learn to solve these problems like regular computational programs like computing loan interest or tax rebates. Solutions to problems that cannot be programmed inherently need a different approach where we use the data itself to drive decisions instead of using programmable logic, rules, or code to make these decisions. We discuss this further in future sections.

Efficiency and Scale

While getting insights and making decisions driven by data are of paramount importance, it also needs to be done with efficiency and at scale. The key idea of using techniques from Machine Learning or artificial intelligence is to automate processes or tasks by learning specific patterns from the data. We all want computers or machines to tell us when a stock might rise or fall, whether an image is of a computer or a television, whether our product placement and offers are the best, determine shopping price trends, detect failures or outages before they occur, and the list just goes on! While human intelligence and expertise is something that we definitely can't do without, we need to solve real-world problems at huge scale with efficiency.

Why Machine Learning?

We will now address the question that started this discussion of why we need Machine Learning. Considering what you have learned so far, while the traditional programming paradigm is quite good and human intelligence and domain expertise is definitely an important factor in making data-driven decisions, we need Machine Learning to make faster and better decisions. The Machine Learning paradigm tries to take into account data and expected outputs or results if any and uses the computer to build the program, which is also known as a model. This program or model can then be used in the future to make necessary decisions and give expected outputs from new inputs. the Machine Learning paradigm is similar yet different from traditional programming paradigms.

The Machine Learning paradigm, the machine, in this context the computer, tries to use input data and expected outputs to try to learn inherent patterns in the data that would ultimately help in building a model analogous to a computer program, which would help in making data-driven decisions in the future (predict or tell us the output) for new input data points by using the learned knowledge from previous data points (its knowledge or experience). You might start to see the benefit in this. We would not need hand-coded rules, complex flowcharts, case and if-then conditions, and other criteria that are typically used to build any decision making system or a decision support system. The basic idea is to use Machine Learning to make insightful decisions.

In the traditional programming approach, we talked about hiring new staff, setting up rule-based monitoring systems, and so on. If we were to use a Machine Learning paradigm shift here, we could go about solving the problem using the following steps.

• Leverage device data and logs and make sure we have enough historical data in some data store (database, logs, or flat files)

- Decide key data attributes that could be useful for building a model. This could be device usage, logs, memory, processor, connections, line strength, links, and so on.

- Observe and capture device attributes and their behavior over various time periods that would include normal device behavior and anomalous device behavior or outages. These outcomes would be your outputs and device data would be your inputs

- Feed these input and output pairs to any specific Machine Learning algorithm in your computer and build a model that learns inherent device patterns and observes the corresponding output or outcome

- Deploy this model such that for newer values of device attributes it can predict if a specific device is behaving normally or it might cause a potential outage Thus once you are able to build a Machine Learning model, you can easily deploy it and build an intelligent system around it such that you can not only monitor devices reactively but you would be able to proactively identify potential problems and even fix them before any issues crop up. Imagine building self-heal or auto-heal systems coupled with round the clock device monitoring. The possibilities are indeed endless and you will not have to keep on hiring new staff every time you expand your office or buy new infrastructure. Of course, the workflow discussed earlier with the series of steps needed for building a Machine Learning model is much more complex than how it has been portrayed, but again this is just to emphasize and make you think more conceptually rather than technically of how the paradigm has shifted in case of Machine Learning processes and you need to change your thinking too from the traditional based approaches toward being more data-driven. The beauty of Machine Learning is that it is never domain constrained and you can use techniques to solve problems spanning multiple domains, businesses, and industries. you always do not need output data points to build a model; sometimes input data is sufficient (or rather output data might not be present) for techniques more suited toward unsupervised learning (which we will discuss in depth later on in this chapter). A simple example is trying to determine customer shopping patterns by looking at the grocery items they typically buy together in a store based on past transactional data. In the next section, we take a deeper dive toward understanding Machine Learning.

Building Machine Intelligence

The objective of Machine Learning, data mining, or artificial intelligence is to make our lives easier, automate tasks, and take better decisions. Building machine intelligence involves everything we have learned until now starting from Machine Learning concepts to actually implementing and building models and using them in the real world. Machine intelligence can be built using non-traditional computing approaches like Machine Learning. In this section, we establish full-fledged end-to-end Machine Learning pipelines based on the CRISP-DM model, which will help us solve real-world problems by building machine intelligence using a structured process.

Machine Learning Pipelines

The best way to solve a real-world Machine Learning or analytics problem is to use a Machine Learning pipeline starting from getting your data to transforming it into information and insights using Machine Learning algorithms and techniques. This is more of a technical or solution based pipeline and it assumes that several aspects of the CRISP-DM model are already covered, including the following points.

- Business and data understanding

- ML/DM technique selection

- Risk, assumptions, and constraints assessment

A Machine Learning pipeline will mainly consist of elements related to data retrieval and extraction, preparation, modeling, evaluation, and deployment. The major steps in the pipeline are briefly mentioned here.

- **Data retrieval:** This is mainly data collection, extraction, and acquisition from various data sources and data stores.

- **Data preparation:** In this step, we pre-process the data, clean it, wrangle it, and manipulate it as needed. Initial exploratory data analysis is also carried out. Next steps involved extracting, engineering, and selecting features/attributes from the data.

• **Data processing and wrangling:** Mainly concerned with data processing, cleaning, munging, wrangling and performing initial descriptive and exploratory data analysis.

• **Feature extraction and engineering:** Here, we extract important features or attributes from the raw data and even create or engineer new features from existing features.

• **Feature scaling and selection:** Data features often need to be normalized and scaled to prevent Machine Learning algorithms from getting biased. Besides this, often we need to select a subset of all available features based on feature importance and quality.

• **Modeling:** In the process of modeling, we usually feed the data features to a Machine

Learning method or algorithm and train the model, typically to optimize a specific cost function in most cases with the objective of reducing errors and generalizing the representations learned from the data.

• **Model evaluation and tuning:** Built models are evaluated and tested on validation datasets and, based on metrics like accuracy, F1 score, and others, the model performance is evaluated. Models have various parameters that are tuned in a process called hyperparameter optimization to get models with the best and optimal results.

- **Deployment and monitoring:** Selected models are deployed in production and

are constantly monitored based on their predictions and results.

Supervised Machine Learning Pipeline

By now we know that supervised Machine Learning methods are all about working with supervised labeled data to train models and then predict outcomes for new data samples. Some processes like feature engineering, scaling, and selection should always remain constant so that the same features are used for training the model and the same features are extracted from new data samples to feed the model in the prediction phase.

Unsupervised Machine Learning Pipeline

Unsupervised Machine Learning is all about extracting patterns, relationships, associations, and clusters from data. The processes related to feature engineering, scaling and selection are similar to supervised learning. However there is no concept of pre-labeled data here. Hence the unsupervised Machine Learning pipeline would be slightly different in contrast to the supervised pipeline.

CHAPTER TWO

Understanding Machine Learning

By now, you have seen how a typical real-world problem suitable to solve using Machine Learning might look like. Besides this, you have also got a good grasp over the basics of traditional programming and Machine Learning paradigms. In this section, we discuss Machine Learning in more detail. To be more specific, we will look at Machine Learning from a conceptual as well as a domain-specific standpoint.

Machine Learning came into prominence perhaps in the 1990s when researchers and scientists started giving it more prominence as a sub-field of Artificial Intelligence (AI) such that techniques borrow concepts from AI, probability, and statistics, which perform far better compared to using fixed rule-based models requiring a lot of manual time and effort. Of course, as we have pointed out earlier, Machine Learning didn't just come out of nowhere in the 1990s. It is a multi-disciplinary field that has gradually evolved over time and is still evolving as we speak.

A brief mention of history of evolution would be really helpful to get an idea of the various concepts and techniques that have been involved in the development of Machine Learning and AI. You could say that it started off in the late 1700s and the early 1800s when the first works of research were published which basically talked about the Bayes' Theorem. In fact Thomas Bayes' major work, "An Essay Towards Solving a Problem in the Doctrine of Chances," was published in 1763. Besides this, a lot of research and discovery was done during this time in the field of probability and mathematics. This paved the way for more ground breaking research and inventions in the 20th Century, which included Markov Chains by Andrey Markov in the early 1900s, proposition of a learning system by Alan Turing, and the invention of the very famous perceptron by Frank Rosenblatt in the 1950s. Many of you might know that neural networks had several highs and lows since the 1950s and they finally came back to prominence in the 1980s with the discovery of backpropagation (thanks to Rumelhart, Hinton, and Williams!) and several other inventions, including Hopfield networks, neocognition, convolutional and recurrent neural networks, and Q-learning. Of course, rapid strides of evolution started taking place in Machine Learning too since the 1990s with the discovery of random forests, support vector machines, long short-term memory networks (LSTMs), and development and release of frameworks in both machine and Deep Learning including torch, theano, tensorflow, scikit-learn, and so on. We also saw the rise of intelligent systems including IBM Watson, DeepFace, and AlphaGo. Indeed the journey has been quite a roller coaster ride and there's still miles to go in this journey.

Take a moment and reflect on this evolutional journey and let's talk about the purpose of this journey. Why and when should we really make machines learn?

Why Make Machines Learn?

We have discussed a fair bit about why we need Machine Learning in a previous section when we address the issue of trying to leverage data to make data-driven decisions at scale using learning algorithms without focusing too much on manual efforts and fixed rule-based systems. In this section, we discuss in more detail why and when should we make machines learn. There are several real-world tasks and problems that humans, businesses, and organizations try to solve day in and day out for our benefit. There are several scenarios when it might be beneficial to make machines learn and some of them are mentioned as follows:

• Lack of sufficient human expertise in a domain (e.g., simulating navigations in unknown territories or even spatial planets).

• Scenarios and behavior can keep changing over time (e.g., availability of infrastructure in an organization, network connectivity, and so on).

• Humans have sufficient expertise in the domain but it is extremely difficult to formally explain or translate this expertise into computational tasks (e.g., speech recognition, translation, scene recognition, cognitive tasks, and so on).

• Addressing domain specific problems at scale with huge volumes of data with too many complex conditions and constraints.

The previously mentioned scenarios are just several examples where making machines learn would be more effective than investing time, effort, and money in trying to build sub-par intelligent systems that might be limited in scope, coverage, performance, and intelligence. We as humans and domain experts already have enough knowledge about the world and our respective domains, which can be objective, subjective, and sometimes even intuitive. With the availability of large volumes of historical data, we can leverage the Machine Learning paradigm to make machines perform specific tasks by gaining enough experience by observing patterns in data over a period of time and then use this experience in solving tasks in the future with minimal manual intervention. The core idea remains to make machines solve tasks that can be easily defined intuitively and almost involuntarily but extremely hard to define formally.

CHAPTER 3

Data Science

The field of Data Science is a very diverse, inter-disciplinary field which encompasses multiple fields . Data Science basically deals with principles, methodologies, processes, tools, and techniques to gather knowledge or information from data (structured as well as unstructured). Data Science is more of a compilation of processes, techniques, and methodologies to foster a data-driven decision based culture.

Basically there are three major components and Data Science sits at the intersection of them. Math and statistics knowledge is all about applying various computational and quantitative math and statistical based techniques to extract insights from data. Hacking skills basically indicate the capability of handling, processing, manipulating and wrangling data into easy to understand and analyzable formats. Substantive expertise is basically the actual real-world domain expertise which is extremely important when you are solving a problem because you need to know about various factors, attributes, constraints, and knowledge related to the domain besides your expertise in data and algorithms.

Thus Drew rightly points out that Machine Learning is a combination of expertise on data hacking skills, math, and statistical learning methods and for Data Science, you need some level of domain expertise and knowledge along with Machine Learning. You can check out Drew's personal insights in his article at http://drewconway.com/zia/2013/3/26/the-data-science-venn-diagram, where talks all about the Data Science Venn diagram. Besides this, we also have Brendan Tierney, who talks about the true nature of Data Science being a multi-disciplinary field with his own depiction If you observe his depiction closely, you will see a lot of the domains mentioned here. You can clearly see Data Science being the center of attention and drawing parts from all the other fields and Machine Learning as a sub-field.

Statistics

The field of statistics can be defined as a specialized branch of mathematics that consists of frameworks and methodologies to collect, organize, analyze, interpret, and present data. Generally this falls more under applied mathematics and borrows concepts from linear algebra, distributions, probability theory, and inferential methodologies. There are two major areas under statistics that are mentioned as follows.

- Descriptive statistics

- Inferential statistics

The core component of any statistical process is data. Hence typically data collection is done first, which could be in global terms, often called a population or a more restricted subset due to various constraints often knows as a sample. Samples are usually collected manually, from surveys, experiments, data stores, and observational studies. From this data, various analyses are carried out using statistical methods.

Descriptive statistics is used to understand basic characteristics of the data using various aggregation and summarization measures to describe and understand the data better. These could be standard measures like mean, median, mode, skewness, kurtosis, standard deviation, variance, and so on.

You can refer to any standard book on statistics to deep dive into these measures if you're interested. The following snippet depicts how to compute some essential descriptive statistical measures.

In [74]: # descriptive statistics

...: import scipy as sp

...: import numpy as np

...:

...: # get data

...: nums = np.random.randint(1,20, size=(1,15))[0]

...: print('Data: ', nums)

...:

...: # get descriptive stats

...: print ('Mean:', sp.mean(nums))

...: print ('Median:', sp.median(nums))

...: print ('Mode:', sp.stats.mode(nums))

```
...: print ('Standard Deviation:', sp.std(nums))

...: print ('Variance:', sp.var(nums))

...: print ('Skew:', sp.stats.skew(nums))

...: print ('Kurtosis:', sp.stats.kurtosis(nums))

...:
```

Data: [2 19 8 10 17 13 18 9 19 16 4 14 16 15 5]

Mean: 12.3333333333

Median: 14.0

Mode: ModeResult(mode=array([16]), count=array([2]))

Standard Deviation: 5.44875113112

Variance: 29.6888888889

Skew: -0.49820055879944575

Kurtosis: -1.0714842769550714

Libraries and frameworks like pandas, scipy, and numpy in general help us compute descriptive statistics and summarize data easily in Python. Inferential statistics are used when we want to test hypothesis, draw inferences, and conclusions about various characteristics of our data sample or population. Frameworks and techniques like hypothesis testing, correlation, and regression analysis, forecasting, and predictions are typically used for any form of inferential statistics. We look at this in much detail in subsequent chapters when we cover predictive analytics as well as time series based forecasting.

Data Mining

The field of data mining involves processes, methodologies, tools and techniques to discover and extract patterns, knowledge, insights and valuable information from non-trivial datasets. Data sets are defined as non-trivial when they are substantially huge usually available from databases and data warehouses.

Once again, data mining itself is a multi-disciplinary field, incorporating concepts and techniques from mathematics, statistics, computer science, databases, Machine Learning and Data Science. The term is a misnomer in general since the "mining" refers to the mining of actual insights or information from the data and not data itself! In the whole process of KDD or Knowledge Discovery in Databases, data mining is the step where all the analysis takes place.

In general, both KDD as well as data mining are closely linked with Machine Learning since they are all concerned with analyzing data to extract useful patterns and insights. Hence methodologies, concepts, techniques, and processes are shared among them. The standard process for data mining followed in the industry is known as the CRISP-DM model.

Artificial Intelligence

The field of artificial Intelligence encompasses multiple sub-fields including Machine Learning, natural language processing, data mining, and so on. It can be defined as the art, science and engineering of making intelligent agents, machines and programs. The field aims to provide solutions for one simple yet extremely tough objective, "Can machines think, reason, and act like human beings?" AI in fact existed as early as the 1300s when people started asking such questions and conducting research and development on building tools that could work on concepts instead of numbers like a calculator does. Progress in AI took place in a steady pace with discoveries and inventions by Alan Turing, McCullouch, and Pitts Artificial Neurons. AI was revived once again after a slowdown till the 1980s with success of expert systems, the resurgence of neural networks thanks to Hopfield, Rumelhart, McClelland, Hinton, and many more. Faster and better computation thanks to Moore's Law led to fields like data mining, Machine Learning and even Deep Learning come into prominence to solve complex problems that would otherwise have been impossible to solve using traditional approaches.

Some of the main objectives of AI include emulation of cognitive functions also known as cognitive learning, semantics, and knowledge representation, learning, reasoning, problem solving, planning, and natural language processing. AI borrows tools, concepts, and techniques from statistical learning, applied mathematics, optimization methods, logic, probability theory, Machine Learning, data mining, pattern recognition, and linguistics. AI is still evolving over time and a lot of innovation is being done in this field including some of the latest discoveries and inventions like self-driving cars, chatbots, drones, and intelligent robots.

Natural Language Processing

The field of Natural Language Processing (NLP) is a multi-disciplinary field combining concepts from computational linguistics, computer science and artificial intelligence. NLP involves the ability to make machines process, understand, and interact with natural human languages. The major objective of applications or systems built using NLP is to enable interactions between machines and natural languages that have evolved over time. Major challenges in this aspect include knowledge and semantics representation, natural language understanding, generation, and processing. Some of the major applications of NLP are mentioned as follows.

- Machine translation

- Speech recognition

- Question answering systems

- Context recognition and resolution

- Text summarization

- Text categorization

- Information extraction

- Sentiment and emotion analysis

- Topic segmentation

Using techniques from NLP and text analytics, you can work on text data to process, annotate, classify, cluster, summarize, extract semantics, determine sentiment, and much more! The following example snippet depicts some basic NLP operations on textual data where we annotate a document (text sentence) with various components like parts of speech, phrase level tags, and so on based on its constituent grammar.

In [98]: # print the constituency parse tree

...: print(tree)

```
(ROOT

(NP

(NP (DT The) (JJ quick) (JJ brown) (NN fox))

(NP

(NP (NNS jumps))

(PP (IN over) (NP (DT the) (JJ lazy) (NN dog))))))
```

In [99]: # visualize constituency parse tree

...: tree.draw()

The constituency grammar based parse tree for our sample sentence, which consists of multiple noun phrases (NP). Each phrase has several words that are also annotated with their own parts of speech (POS) tags. We cover more on processing and analyzing textual data for various steps in the Machine Learning pipeline as well as practical use cases in subsequent chapters.

Deep Learning

The field of Deep Learning, as depicted earlier, is a sub-field of Machine Learning that has recently come into much prominence. Its main objective is to get Machine Learning research closer to its true goal of "making machines intelligent". Deep Learning is often termed as a rebranded fancy term for neural networks. This is true to some extent but there is definitely more to Deep Learning than just basic neural networks. Deep Learning based algorithms involves the use of concepts from representation learning where various representations of the data are learned in different layers that also aid in automated feature extraction from the data. In simple terms, a Deep Learning based approach tries to build machine intelligence by representing data as a layered hierarchy of concepts, where each layer of concepts is built from other simpler layers. This layered architecture itself is one of the core components of any Deep Learning algorithm.

In any basic supervised Machine Learning technique, we basically try to learn a mapping between our data samples and our output and then try to predict output for newer data samples. Representational learning tries to understand the representations in the data itself besides learning mapping from inputs to outputs. This makes Deep Learning algorithms extremely powerful as compared to regular techniques, which require significant expertise in areas like feature extraction and engineering. Deep Learning is also extremely effective with regard to its performance as well as scalability with more and more data as compared to older Machine Learning algorithms.

Indeed, as rightly pointed out by Andrew Ng, there have been several noticeable trends and characteristics related to Deep Learning that we have noticed over the past decade. They are summarized as follows.

• Deep Learning algorithms are based on distributed representational learning and they start performing better with more data over time.

• Deep Learning could be said to be a rebranding of neural networks, but there is a lot into it compared to traditional neural networks.

• Better software frameworks like tensorflow, theano, caffe, mxnet, and keras, coupled with superior hardware have made it possible to build extremely complex, multi-layered Deep Learning models with huge sizes.

- Deep Learning has multiple advantages related to automated feature extraction as well as performing supervised learning operations, which have helped data scientists and engineers solve increasingly complex problems over time.

The following points describe the salient features of most Deep Learning algorithms, some of which we will be using in this book.

- Hierarchical layered representation of concepts. These concepts are also called features in Machine Learning terminology (data attributes).

- Distributed representational learning of the data happens through a multi-layered architecture (unsupervised learning).

- More complex and high-level features and concepts are derived from simpler, lowlevel features.

- A "deep" neural network usually

- A "deep" neural network usually is considered to have at least more than one hidden layer besides the input and output layers. Usually it consists of a minimum of three to four hidden layers.

- Deep architectures have a multi-layered architecture where each layer consists of multiple non-linear processing units. Each layer's input is the previous layer in the architecture. The first layer is usually the input and the last layer is the output.

- Can perform automated feature extraction, classification, anomaly detection, and many other Machine Learning tasks.

This should give you a good foundational grasp of the concepts pertaining to Deep Learning. Suppose we had a real-world problem of object recognition from images.

You can clearly see how Deep Learning methods involve a hierarchical layer representation of features and concept from the raw data as compared to other Machine Learning methods. We conclude this section with a brief coverage of some essential concepts pertaining to Deep Learning.

Important Concepts

In this section, we discuss some key terms and concepts from Deep Learning algorithms and architecture. This should be useful in the future when you are building your own Deep Learning models.

Artificial Neural Networks

An Artificial Neural Network (ANN) is a computational model and architecture that simulates biological neurons and the way they function in our brain. Typically, an ANN has layers of interconnected nodes. The nodes and their inter-connections are analogous to the network of neurons in our brain.

Any basic ANN will always have multiple layers of nodes, specific connection patterns and links between the layers, connection weights and activation functions for the nodes/neurons that convert weighted inputs to outputs. The process of learning for the network typically involves a cost function and the objective is to optimize the cost function (typically minimize the cost). The weights keep getting updated in the process of learning.

Backpropagation

The backpropagation algorithm is a popular technique to train ANNs and it led to a resurgence in the popularity of neural networks in the 1980s. The algorithm typically has two main stages — propagation and weight updates. They are described briefly as follows.

1. Propagation

a. The input data sample vectors are propagated forward through the neural network to generate the output values from the output layer.

b. Compare the generated output vector with the actual/desired output vector for that input data vector.

c. Compute difference in error at the output units.

d. Backpropagate error values to generate deltas at each node/neuron.

2. Weight Update

a. Compute weight gradients by multiplying the output delta (error) and input activation.

b. Use learning rate to determine percentage of the gradient to be subtracted from original weight and update the weight of the nodes.

These two stages are repeated multiple times with multiple iterations/epochs until we get satisfactory results. Typically backpropagation is used along with optimization algorithms or functions like stochastic gradient descent.

Multilayer Perceptrons

A multilayer perceptron, also known as MLP, is a fully connected, feed-forward artificial neural network with at least three layers (input, output, and at least one hidden layer) where each layer is fully connected to the adjacent layer. Each neuron usually is a non-linear functional processing unit. Backpropagation is typically used to train MLPs and even deep neural nets are MLPs when they have multiple hidden layers. Typically used for supervised Machine Learning tasks like classification. an input layer, an output layer

CHAPTER 4

Machine Learning Methods

Machine Learning has multiple algorithms, techniques, and methodologies that can be used to build models to solve real-world problems using data. This section tries to classify these Machine Learning methods under some broad categories to give some sense to the overall landscape of Machine Learning methods that are ultimately used to perform specific Machine Learning tasks we discussed in a previous section. Typically the same Machine Learning methods can be classified in multiple ways under multiple umbrellas. Following are some of the major broad areas of Machine Learning methods.

1. Methods based on the amount of human supervision in the learning process

a. Supervised learning

b. Unsupervised learning

c. Semi-supervised learning

d. Reinforcement learning

2. Methods based on the ability to learn from incremental data samples

a. Batch learning

b. Online learning

3. Methods based on their approach to generalization from data samples

a. Instance based learning

b. Model based learning

We briefly cover the various types of learning methods in the following sections to build a good foundation with regard to Machine Learning methods and the type of tasks they usually solve. This should give you enough knowledge to start understanding which methods should be applied in what scenarios when we tackle various real-world use cases and problems in the subsequent chapters of the book.

Supervised Learning

Supervised learning methods or algorithms include learning algorithms that take in data samples (known as training data) and associated outputs (known as labels or responses) with each data sample during the model training process. The main objective is to learn a mapping or association between input data samples x and their corresponding outputs y based on multiple training data instances. This learned knowledge can then be used in the future to predict an output y' for any new input data sample x' which was previously unknown or unseen during the model training process. These methods are termed as supervised because the model learns on data samples where the desired output responses/labels are already known beforehand in the training phase.

Supervised learning basically tries to model the relationship between the inputs and their corresponding outputs from the training data so that we would be able to predict output responses for new data inputs based on the knowledge it gained earlier with regard to relationships and mappings between the inputs and their target outputs. This is precisely why supervised learning methods are extensively used in predictive analytics where the main objective is to predict some response for some input data that's typically fed into a trained supervised ML model. Supervised learning methods are of two major classes based on the type of ML tasks they aim to solve.

- Classification

- Regression

Let's look at these two Machine Learning tasks and observe the subset of supervised learning methods that are best suited for tackling these tasks.

Classification

The classification based tasks are a sub-field under supervised Machine Learning, where the key objective is to predict output labels or responses that are categorical in nature for input data based on what the model has learned in the training phase. Output labels here are also known as classes or class labels are these are categorical in nature meaning they are unordered and discrete values. Thus, each output response belongs to a specific discrete class or category.

Suppose we take a real-world example of predicting the weather. Let's keep it simple and say we are trying to predict if the weather is sunny or rainy based on multiple input data samples consisting of attributes or features like humidity, temperature, pressure, and precipitation. Since the prediction can be either sunny or rainy, there are a total of two distinct classes in total; hence this problem can also be termed as a binary classification problem.

A task where the total number of distinct classes is more than two becomes a multi-class classification problem where each prediction response can be any one of the probable classes from this set. A simple example would be trying to predict numeric digits from scanned handwritten images. In this case it becomes a 10-class classification problem because the output class label for any image can be any digit from 0 - 9. In both the cases, the output class is a scalar value pointing to one specific class. Multi-label classification tasks are such that based on any input data sample, the output response is usually a vector having one or more than one output class label. A simple real-world problem would be trying to predict the category of a news article that could have multiple output classes like news, finance, politics, and so on.

Popular classification algorithms include logistic regression, support vector machines, neural networks, ensembles like random forests and gradient boosting, K-nearest neighbors, decision trees, and many more.

Regression

Machine Learning tasks where the main objective is value estimation can be termed as regression tasks. Regression based methods are trained on input data samples having output responses that are continuous numeric values unlike classification, where we have discrete categories or classes. Regression models make use of input data attributes or features (also called explanatory or independent variables) and their corresponding continuous numeric output values (also called as response, dependent, or outcome variable) to learn specific relationships and associations between the inputs and their corresponding outputs. With this knowledge, it can predict output responses for new, unseen data instances similar to classification but with continuous numeric outputs.

One of the most common real-world examples of regression is prediction of house prices. You can build a simple regression model to predict house prices based on data pertaining to land plot areas in square feet. The basic idea here is that we try to determine if there is any relationship or association between the data feature plot area and the outcome variable, which is the house price and is what we want to predict.

Simple linear regression models try to model relationships on data with one feature or explanatory variable x and a single response variable y where the objective is to predict y. Methods like ordinary least squares (OLS) are typically used to get the best linear fit during model training.

Multiple regression is also known as multivariable regression. These methods try to model data where we have one response output variable y in each observation but multiple explanatory variables in the form of a vector X instead of a single explanatory variable. The idea is to predict y based on the different features present in X. A real-world example would be extending our house prediction model to build a more sophisticated model where we predict the house price based on multiple features instead of just plot area in each data sample. The features could be represented in a vector as plot area, number of bedrooms, number of bathrooms, total floors, furnished, or unfurnished. Based on all these attributes, the model tries to learn the relationship between each feature vector and its corresponding house price so that it can predict them in the future. Polynomial regression is a special case of multiple regression where the response variable y is modeled as an nth degree polynomial of the input feature x. Basically it is multiple regression, where each feature in the input feature vector is a multiple of x.

Non-linear regression methods try to model relationships between input features and outputs based on a combination of non-linear functions applied on the input features and necessary model parameters.

Lasso regression is a special form of regression that performs normal regression and generalizes the model well by performing regularization as well as feature or variable selection. Lasso stands for least absolute shrinkage and selection operator. The L1 norm is typically used as the regularization term in lasso regression.

Ridge regression is another special form of regression that performs normal regression and generalizes the model by performing regularization to prevent overfitting the model. Typically the L2 norm is used as the regularization term in ridge regression.

Generalized linear models are generic frameworks that can be used to model data predicting different types of output responses, including continuous, discrete, and ordinal data. Algorithms like logistic regression are used for categorical data and ordered probit regression for ordinal data.

Unsupervised Learning

Supervised learning methods usually require some training data where the outcomes which we are trying to predict are already available in the form of discrete labels or continuous values. However, often we do not have the liberty or advantage of having pre-labeled training data and we still want to extract useful insights or patterns from our data. In this scenario, unsupervised learning methods are extremely powerful. These methods are called unsupervised because the model or algorithm tries to learn inherent latent structures, patterns and relationships from given data without any help or supervision like providing annotations in the form of labeled outputs or outcomes.

Unsupervised learning is more concerned with trying to extract meaningful insights or information from data rather than trying to predict some outcome based on previously available supervised training data. There is more uncertainty in the results of unsupervised learning but you can also gain a lot of information from these models that was previously unavailable to view just by looking at the raw data.

Often unsupervised learning could be one of the tasks involved in building a huge intelligence system. For example, we could use unsupervised learning to get possible outcome labels for tweet sentiments by using the knowledge of the English vocabulary and then train a supervised model on similar data points and their outcomes which we obtained previously through unsupervised learning. There is no hard and fast rule with regard to using just one specific technique. You can always combine multiple methods as long as they are relevant in solving the problem. Unsupervised learning methods can be categorized under the following broad areas of ML tasks relevant to unsupervised learning.

- Clustering

- Dimensionality reduction

- Anomaly detection

- Association rule-mining

We explore these tasks briefly in the following sections to get a good feel of how unsupervised learning methods are used in the real world.

Clustering

Clustering methods are Machine Learning methods that try to find patterns of similarity and relationships among data samples in our dataset and then cluster these samples into various groups, such that each group or cluster of data samples has some similarity, based on the inherent attributes or features. These methods are completely unsupervised because they try to cluster data by looking at the data features without any prior training, supervision, or knowledge about data attributes, associations, and relationships.

Consider a real-world problem of running multiple servers in a data center and trying to analyze logs for typical issues or errors. Our main task is to determine the various kinds of log messages that usually occur frequently each week. In simple words, we want to group log messages into various clusters based on some inherent characteristics. A simple approach would be to extract features from the log messages, which would be in textual format and apply clustering on the same and group similar log messages together based on similarity in content.

Basically we have raw log messages to start with. Our clustering system would employ feature extraction to extract features from text like word occurrences, phrase occurrences, and so on. Finally, a clustering algorithm like K-means or hierarchical clustering would be employed to group or cluster messages based on similarity of their inherent features.

Dimensionality Reduction

Once we start extracting attributes or features from raw data samples, sometimes our feature space gets bloated up with a humongous number of features. This poses multiple challenges including analyzing and visualizing data with thousands or millions of features, which makes the feature space extremely complex posing problems with regard to training models, memory, and space constraints. In fact this is referred to as the "curse of dimensionality". Unsupervised methods can also be used in these scenarios, where we reduce the number of features or attributes for each data sample. These methods reduce the number of feature variables by extracting or selecting a set of principal or representative features. There are multiple popular algorithms available for dimensionality reduction like Principal Component Analysis (PCA), nearest neighbors, and discriminant analysis. Dimensionality reduction techniques can be classified in two major approaches as follows.

• **Feature Selection methods:** Specific features are selected for each data sample from the original list of features and other features are discarded. No new features are generated in this process.

• **Feature Extraction methods:** We engineer or extract new features from the original list of features in the data. Thus the reduced subset of features will contain newly generated features that were not part of the original feature set. PCA falls under this category.

Anomaly Detection

The process of anomaly detection is also termed as outlier detection, where we are interested in finding out occurrences of rare events or observations that typically do not occur normally based on historical data samples. Sometimes anomalies occur infrequently and are thus rare events, and in other instances, anomalies might not be rare but might occur in very short bursts over time, thus have specific patterns.

Unsupervised learning methods can be used for anomaly detection such that we train the algorithm on the training dataset having normal, non-anomalous data samples. Once it learns the necessary data representations, patterns, and relations among attributes in normal samples, for any new data sample, it would be able to identify it as anomalous or a normal data point by using its learned knowledge.

Anomaly detection based methods are extremely popular in real-world scenarios like detection of security attacks or breaches, credit card fraud, manufacturing anomalies, network issues, and many more.

Semi-Supervised Learning

The semi-supervised learning methods typically fall between supervised and unsupervised learning methods. These methods usually use a lot of training data that's unlabeled (forming the unsupervised learning component) and a small amount of pre-labeled and annotated data (forming the supervised learning component). Multiple techniques are available in the form of generative methods, graph based methods, and heuristic based methods.

A simple approach would be building a supervised model based on labeled data, which is limited, and then applying the same to large amounts of unlabeled data to get more labeled samples, train the model on them and repeat the process. Another approach would be to use unsupervised algorithms to cluster similar data samples, use human-in-the-loop efforts to manually annotate or label these groups, and then use a combination of this information in the future. This approach is used in many image tagging systems.

CHAPTER 5

Reinforcement Learning

The reinforcement learning methods are a bit different from conventional supervised or unsupervised methods. In this context, we have an agent that we want to train over a period of time to interact with a specific environment and improve its performance over a period of time with regard to the type of actions it performs on the environment. Typically the agent starts with a set of strategies or policies for interacting with the environment. On observing the environment, it takes a particular action based on a rule or policy and by observing the current state of the environment. Based on the action, the agent gets a reward, which could be beneficial or detrimental in the form of a penalty. It updates its current policies and strategies if needed and this iterative process continues till it learns enough about its environment to get the desired rewards. The main steps of a reinforcement learning method are mentioned as follows.

1. Prepare agent with set of initial policies and strategy

2. Observe environment and current state

3. Select optimal policy and perform action

4. Get corresponding reward (or penalty)

5. Update policies if needed

6. Repeat Steps 2 - 5 iteratively until agent learns the most optimal policies

Consider a real-world problem of trying to make a robot or a machine learn to play chess. In this case the agent would be the robot and the environment and states would be the chessboard and the positions of the chess pieces.

Batch Learning

Batch learning methods are also popularly known as offline learning methods. These are Machine Learning methods that are used in end-to-end Machine Learning systems where the model is trained using all the available training data in one go. Once training is done and the model completes the process of learning, on getting a satisfactory performance, it is deployed into production where it predicts outputs for new data samples. However, the model doesn't keep learning over a period of time continuously with the new data.

Once the training is complete the model stops learning. Thus, since the model trains with data in one single batch and it is usually a one-time procedure, this is known as batch or offline learning.

Online Learning

Online learning methods work in a different way as compared to batch learning methods. The training data is usually fed in multiple incremental batches to the algorithm. These data batches are also known as mini-batches in ML terminology. However, the training process does not end there unlike batch learning methods. It keeps on learning over a period of time based on new data samples which are sent to it for prediction. Basically it predicts and learns in the process with new data on the fly without have to re-run the whole model on previous data samples.

There are several advantages to online learning — it is suitable in real-world scenarios where the model might need to keep learning and re-training on new data samples as they arrive. Problems like device failure or anomaly prediction and stock market forecasting are two relevant scenarios. Besides this, since the data is fed to the model in incremental mini-batches, you can build these models on commodity hardware without worrying about memory or disk constraints since unlike batch learning methods, you do not need to load the full dataset in memory before training the model. Besides this, once the model trains on datasets, you can remove them since we do not need the same data again as the model learns incrementally and remembers what it has learned in the past.

One of the major caveats in online learning methods is the fact that bad data samples can affect the model performance adversely. All ML methods work on the principle of "Garbage In Garbage Out". Hence if you supply bad data samples to a well-trained model, it can start learning relationships and patterns that have no real significance and this ends up affecting the overall model performance. Since online learning methods keep learning based on new data samples, you should ensure proper checks are in place to notify you in case suddenly the model performance drops. Also suitable model parameters like learning rate should be selected with care to ensure the model doesn't overfit or get biased based on specific data samples.

Instance Based Learning

There are various ways to build Machine Learning models using methods that try to generalize based on input data. Instance based learning involves ML systems and methods that use the raw data points themselves to figure out outcomes for newer, previously unseen data samples instead of building an explicit model on training data and then testing it out.

A simple example would be a K-nearest neighbor algorithm. Assuming k = 3, we have our initial training data. The ML method knows the representation of the data from the features, including its dimensions, position of each data point, and so on. For any new data point, it will use a similarity measure (like cosine or Euclidean distance) and find the three nearest input data points to this new data point. Once that is decided, we simply take a majority of the outcomes for those three training points and predict or assign it as the outcome label/response for this new data point. Thus, instance based learning works by looking at the input data points and using a similarity metric to generalize and predict for new data points.

The model based learning methods are a more traditional ML approach toward generalizing based on training data. Typically an iterative process takes place where the input data is used to extract features and models are built based on various model parameters (known as hyperparameters). These hyperparameters are optimized based on various model validation techniques to select the model that generalizes best on the training data and some amount of validation and test data (split from the initial dataset). Finally, the best model is used to make predictions or decisions as and when needed.

The CRISP-DM Process Model

The CRISP-DM model stands for CRoss Industry Standard Process for Data Mining. More popularly known by the acronym itself, CRISP-DM is a tried, tested, and robust industry standard process model followed for data mining and analytics projects. CRISP-DM clearly depicts necessary steps, processes, and workflows for executing any project right from formalizing business requirements to testing and deploying a solution to transform data into insights. Data Science, Data Mining, and Machine Learning are all about trying to run multiple iterative processes to extract insights and information from data. Hence we can say that analyzing data is truly both an art as well as a science, because it is not always about running algorithms without reason; a lot of the major effort involves in understanding the business, the actual value of the efforts being invested, and proper methods to articulate end results and insights.

The CRISP-DM model tells us that for building an end-to-end solution for any analytics project or system, there are a total of six major steps or phases, some of them being iterative. Just like we have a software development lifecycle with several major phases or steps for a software development project, we have a data mining or analysis lifecycle in this scenario.

CHAPTER 6

The Python Machine Learning Ecosystem

Machine Learning is a very popular and relevant topic in the world of technology today. Hence we have a very diverse and varied support for Machine Learning in terms of programming languages and frameworks. There are Machine Learning libraries for almost all popular languages including C++, R, Julia, Scala, Python, etc. In this chapter we try to justify why Python is an apt language for Machine Learning. Once we have argued our selection logically, we give you a brief introduction to the Python Machine Learning (ML) ecosystem. This Python ML ecosystem is a collection of libraries that enable the developers to extract and transform data, perform data wrangling operations, apply existing robust Machine Learning algorithms and also develop custom algorithms easily. These libraries include numpy, scipy, pandas, scikit-learn, statsmodels, tensorflow, keras, and so on. We cover several of these libraries in a nutshell so that the user will have some familiarity with the basics of each of these libraries. These will be used extensively in the later chapters of the book. An important thing to keep in mind here is that the purpose of this chapter is to acquaint you with the diverse set of frameworks and libraries in the Python ML ecosystem to get an idea of what can be leveraged to solve Machine Learning problems. We enrich the content with useful links that you can refer to for extensive documentation and tutorials. We assume some basic proficiency with Python and programming in general. All the code snippets and examples used in this chapter is available in the GitHub repository for this book at https://github.com/dipanjanS/practicalmachine-learning-with-python under the directory. named python_ml_ecosystem.py for all the examples used in this chapter and try the examples as you read this chapter or you can even refer to the jupyter notebook named The Python Machine Learning Ecosystem.ipynb for a more interactive experience.

Python: An Introduction

Python was created by Guido van Rossum at Stichting Mathematisch Centrum (CWI, see https://www.cwi.nl/) in the Netherlands. The first version of Python was released in 1991. Guido wrote Python as a successor of the language called ABC. In the following years Python has developed into an extensively used high level language and a general programming language. Python is an interpreted language, which means that the source code of a Python program is converted into bytecode, which is then executed by the Python virtual machine. Python is The Python Machine Learning Ecosystem Machine Learning is a very popular and relevant topic in the world of technology today. Hence we have a very diverse and varied support for Machine Learning in terms of programming languages and frameworks. There are Machine Learning libraries for almost all popular languages including C++, R, Julia, Scala, Python, etc. In this chapter we try to justify why Python is an apt language for Machine Learning. Once we have argued our selection logically, we give you a brief introduction to the Python Machine Learning (ML) ecosystem. This Python ML ecosystem is a collection of libraries that enable the developers to extract and transform data, perform data wrangling operations, apply existing robust Machine Learning algorithms and also develop custom algorithms easily. These libraries include numpy, scipy, pandas, scikit-learn, statsmodels, tensorflow, keras, and so on. We cover several of these libraries in a nutshell so that the user will have some familiarity with the basics of each of these libraries. These will be used extensively in the later chapters of the book. An important thing to keep in mind here is that the purpose of this chapter is to acquaint you with the diverse set of frameworks and libraries in the Python ML ecosystem to get an idea of what can be leveraged to solve Machine Learning problems. We enrich the content with useful links that you can refer to for extensive documentation and tutorials.

Python was created by Guido van Rossum at Stichting Mathematisch Centrum (CWI, see https://www.cwi.nl/) in the Netherlands. The first version of Python was released in 1991. Guido wrote Python as a successor of the language called ABC. In the following years Python has developed into an extensively used high level language and a general programming language. Python is an interpreted language, which means that the source code of a Python program is converted into bytecode, which is then executed by the Python virtual machine. Python is different from major compiled languages like C and C++ as Python code is not required to be built and linked like code for these languages. This distinction makes for two important points:

- **Python code is fast to develop:** As the code is not required to be compiled and built, Python code can be much readily changed and executed. This makes for a fast development cycle.

- **Python code is not as fast in execution:** Since the code is not directly compiled and executed and an additional layer of the Python virtual machine is responsible for execution, Python code runs a little slow as compared to conventional languages like C, C++, etc.

Strengths

Python has steadily risen in the charts of widely used programming languages and according to several surveys and research; it is the fifth most important language in the world. Recently several surveys depicted Python to be the most popular language for Machine Learning and Data Science! We will compile a brief list of advantages that Python offers that probably explains its popularity.

1. Easy to learn: Python is a relatively easy-to-learn language. Its syntax is simple for a beginner to learn and understand. When compared with languages likes C or Java, there is minimal boilerplate code required in executing a Python program.

2. Supports multiple programming paradigms: Python is a multi-paradigm, multi-purpose programming language. It supports object oriented programming, structured programming, functional programming, and even aspect oriented programming. This versatility allows it to be used by a multitude of programmers.

3. Extensible: Extensibility of Python is one of its most important characteristics. Python has a huge number of modules easily available which can be readily installed and used. These modules cover every aspect of programming from data access to implementation of popular algorithms. This easy-to-extend feature ensures that a Python developer is more productive as a large array of problems can be solved by available libraries.

4. Active open source community: Python is open source and supported by a large developer community. This makes it robust and adaptive. The bugs encountered are easily fixed by the Python community. Being open source, developers can tinker with the Python source code if their requirements call for it.

Pitfalls

Although Python is a very popular programming language, it comes with its own share of pitfalls. One of the most important limitations it suffers is in terms of execution speed. Being an interpreted language, it is slow when compared to compiled languages. This limitation can be a bit restrictive in scenarios where extremely high performance code is required. This is a major area of improvement for future implementations of Python and every subsequent Python version addresses it. Although we have to admit it can never be as fast as a compiled language, we are convinced that it makes up for this deficiency by being super-efficient and effective in other departments.

Setting Up a Python Environment

The starting step for our journey into the world of Data Science is the setup of our Python environment. We usually have two options for setting up our environment:

• Install Python and the necessary libraries individually

• Use a pre-packaged Python distribution that comes with necessary libraries, i.e.

Anaconda

Anaconda is a packaged compilation of Python along with a whole suite of a variety of libraries, including core libraries which are widely used in Data Science. Developed by Anaconda, formerly known as Continuum Analytics, it is often the go-to setup for data scientists. Travis Oliphant, primary contributor to both the numpy and scipy libraries, is Anaconda's president and one of the co-founders. The Anaconda distribution is BSD licensed and hence it allows us to use it for commercial and redistribution purposes.

A major advantage of this distribution is that we don't require an elaborate setup and it works well on all flavors of operating systems and platforms, especially Windows, which can often cause problems with installing specific Python packages. Thus, we can get started with our Data Science journey with just one download and install. The Anaconda distribution is widely used across industry Data Science environments and it also comes with a wonderful IDE, Spyder (Scientific Python Development Environment), besides other useful utilities like jupyter notebooks, the IPython console, and the excellent package management tool, conda. Recently they have also talked extensively about Jupyterlab, the next generation UI for Project Jupyter. We recommend using the Anaconda distribution and also checking out https://www.anaconda. com/what-is-anaconda/ to learn more about Anaconda.

Set Up Anaconda Python Environment

The first step in setting up your environment with the required Anaconda distribution is downloading the required installation package from https://www.anaconda.com/download/, which is the provider of the Anaconda distribution. The important point to note here is that we will be using Python 3.5 and the corresponding Anaconda distribution. Python 3.5.2 was released on June 2016 compared to 3.6, which released on December 2016. We have opted for 3.5 as we want to ensure that none of the libraries that we will be using in this book have any compatibility issues. Hence, as Python 3.5 has been around for a long time we avoid any such compatibility issues by opting for it. However, you are free to use Python 3.6 and the code used in this book is expected to work without major issues. We chose to leave out Python 2.7 since support for Python 2 will be ending in 2020 and from the Python community vision, it is clear that Python 3 is the future and we recommend you use it. Download the Anaconda3-4.2.0-Windows-x86_64 package (the one with Python 3.5) from https:// repo.continuum.io/archive/. A screenshot of the target page is shown in Figure 2-1. We have chosen the Windows OS specifically because sometimes, few Python packages or libraries cause issues with installing or running and hence we wanted to make sure we cover those details. If you are using any other OS like Linux or MacOSX, download the correct version for your OS and install it.

Set Up Anaconda Python Environment

The first step in setting up your environment with the required Anaconda distribution is downloading the required installation package from https://www.anaconda.com/download/, which is the provider of the

Anaconda distribution. The important point to note here is that we will be using Python 3.5 and the corresponding Anaconda distribution. Python 3.5.2 was released on June 2016 compared to 3.6, which released on December 2016. We have opted for 3.5 as we want to ensure that none of the libraries that we will be using in this book have any compatibility issues. Hence, as Python 3.5 has been around for a long time we avoid any such compatibility issues by opting for it. However, you are free to use Python 3.6 and the code used in this book is expected to work without major issues. We chose to leave out Python 2.7 since support for Python 2 will be ending in 2020 and from the Python community vision, it is clear that Python 3 is the future and we recommend you use it. Download the Anaconda3-4.2.0-Windows-x86_64 package (the one with Python 3.5) from https://repo.continuum.io/archive/. We have chosen the Windows OS specifically because sometimes, few Python packages or libraries cause issues with installing or running and hence we wanted to make sure we cover those details. If you are using any other OS like Linux or MacOSX, download the correct version for your OS and install it.

Installing the downloaded file is as simple as double-clicking the file and letting the installer take care of the entire process. To check if the installation was successful, just open a command prompt or terminal and start up Python. We also recommend that you use the iPython shell (the command is ipython) instead of the regular Python shell, because you get a lot of features including inline plots, autocomplete, and so on. This should complete the process of setting up your Python environment for Data Science and Machine Learning.

Installing Libraries

We will not be covering the basics of Python, as we assume you are already acquainted with basic Python syntax. Feel free to check out any standard course or book on Python programming to pick up on the basics.

We will cover one very basic but very important aspect of installing additional libraries. In Python the preferred way to install additional libraries is using the pip installer. The basic syntax to install a package from Python Package Index (PyPI) using pip is as follows. pip install required_package.

This will install the required_package if it is present in PyPI. We can also use other sources other than PyPI to install packages but that generally would not be required. The Anaconda distribution is already supplemented with a plethora of additional libraries, hence it is very unlikely that we will need additional packages from other sources.

Another way to install packages, limited to Anaconda, is to use the conda install command. This will install the packages from the Anaconda package channels and usually we recommend using this, especially on Windows.

Why Python for Data Science?

According to a 2017 survey by StackOverflow (https://insights.stackoverflow.com/survey/2017), Python is world's 5th most used language. It is one of the top three languages used by data scientists and one of the most "wanted" language among StackOverflow users. In fact, in a recent poll by KDnuggets in 2017, Python got the maximum number of votes for being the leading platform for Analytics, Data Science, and Machine Learning based on the choice of users (http://www.kdnuggets.com/2017/08/python-overtakesr-leader-analytics-data-science.html).

Python has a lot of advantages that makes it a language of choice when it comes to the practices of Data Science. We will now try to illustrate these advantages and argue our case for "Why Python is a language of choice for Data scientists?"

Powerful Set of Packages

Python is known for its extensive and powerful set of packages. In fact one of the philosophies shared by Python is batteries included, which means that Python has a rich and powerful set of packages ready to be used in a wide variety of domains and use cases. This philosophy is extended into the packages required for Data Science and Machine Learning. Packages like numpy, scipy, pandas, scikit-learn, etc., which are tailor-made for solving a variety of real-world Data Science problems, and are immensely powerful. This makes Python a go-to language for solving Data Science related problems.

Easy and Rapid Prototyping

Python's simplicity is another important aspect when we want to discuss its suitability for Data Science.

Python syntax is easy to understand as well as idiomatic, which makes comprehending existing code a relatively simple task. This allows the developer to easily modify existing implementations and develop his own ones. This feature is especially useful for developing new algorithms which may be experimental or yet to be supported by any external library. Based on what we discussed earlier, Python development is independent of time consuming build and link processes. Using the REPL shell, IDEs, and notebooks, you can rapidly build and iterate over multiple research and development cycles and all the changes can be readily made and tested.

Easy to Collaborate

Data science solutions are rarely a one man job. Often a lot of collaboration is required in a Data Science team to develop a great analytical solution. Luckily Python provides tools that make it extremely easy to collaborate for a diverse team. One of the most liked features, which empowers this collaboration, are jupyter notebooks. Notebooks are a novel concept that allow data scientists to share the code, data, and insightful results in a single place. This makes for an easily reproducible research tool. We consider this to be a very important feature and will devote an entire section to cover the advantages offered by the use of notebooks.

One-Stop Solution

In the first chapter we explored how Data Science as a field is interconnected to various domains. A typical project will have an iterative lifecycle that will involve data extraction, data manipulation, data analysis, feature engineering, modeling, evaluation, solution development, deployment, and continued updating of the solution. Python as a multi-purpose programming language is extremely diverse and it allows developers to address all these assorted operations from a common platform. Using Python libraries you can consume data from a multitude of sources, apply different data wrangling operations to that data, apply Machine Learning algorithms on the processed data, and deploy the developed solution. This makes Python extremely useful as no interface is required, i.e. you don't need to port any part of the whole pipeline to some different programming language. Also enterprise level Data Science projects often require interfacing with different programming languages, which is also achievable by using Python. For example, suppose some enterprise uses a custom made Java library for some esoteric data manipulation, then you can use Jython implementation of Python to use that Java library without writing custom code for the interfacing layer.

Large and Active Community Support

The Python developer community is very active and humongous in number. This large community ensures that the core Python language and packages remain efficient and bug free. A developer can seek support about a Python issue using a variety of platforms like the Python mailing list, stack overflow, blogs, and usenet groups. This large support ecosystem is also one of the reasons for making Python a favored language for Data Science.

Introducing the Python Machine Learning Ecosystem

In this section, we address the important components of the Python Machine Learning ecosystem and give a small introduction to each of them. These components are few of the reasons why Python is an important language for Data Science. This section is structured to give you a gentle introduction and acquaint you with these core Data Science libraries. Covering all of them in depth would be impractical and beyond the current scope since we would be using them in detail in subsequent chapters. Another advantage of having a great community of Python developers is the rich content that can be found about each one of these libraries with a simple search. The list of components that we cover is by no means exhaustive but we have shortlisted them on the basis of their importance in the whole ecosystem.

Jupyter Notebooks

Jupyter notebooks, formerly known as ipython notebooks, are an interactive computational environment that can be used to develop Python based Data Science analyses, which emphasize on reproducible research.

The interactive environment is great for development and enables us to easily share the notebook and hence the code among peers who can replicate our research and analyses by themselves. These jupyter notebooks can contain code, text, images, output, etc., and can be arranged in a step by step manner to give a complete step by step illustration of the whole analysis process. This capability makes notebooks a valuable tool for reproducible analyses and research, especially when you want to share your work with a peer. While developing your analyses, you can document your thought process and capture the results as part of the notebook. This seamless intertwining of documentation, code, and results make jupyter notebooks a valuable tool for every data scientist.

We will be using jupyter notebooks, which are installed by default with our Anaconda distribution. This is similar to the ipython shell with the difference that it can be used for different programming backends, i.e. not just Python. But the functionality is similar for both of these with the added advantage of displaying interactive visualizations and much more on jupyter notebooks.

Installation and Execution

We don't require any additional installation for Jupyter notebooks, as it is already installed by the Anaconda distribution. We can invoke the jupyter notebook by executing the following command at the command prompt or terminal.

C:\>jupyter notebook

This will start a notebook server at the address localhost:8888 of your machine. An important point to note here is that you access the notebook using a browser so you can even initiate it on a remote server and use it locally using techniques like ssh tunneling. This feature is extremely useful in case you have a powerful computing resource that you can only access remotely but lack a GUI for it. Jupyter notebook allows you to access those resources in a visually interactive shell. Once you invoke this command, you can navigate to the address localhost:8888 in your browser. On the landing page we can initiate a new notebook by clicking the New button on top right. By default it will use the default kernel (i.e., the Python 3.5 kernel) but we can also associate the notebook with a different kernel (for example a Python 2.7 kernel, if installed in your system). A notebook is just a collection of cells. There are three major types of cells in a notebook:

1. Code cells: Just like the name suggests, these are the cells that you can use to write your code and associated comments. The contents of these cells are sent to the kernel associated with the notebook and the computed outputs are displayed as the cells' outputs.

2. Markdown cells: Markdown can be used to intelligently notate the computation process. These can contain simple text comments, HTML tags, images, and even Latex equations. These will come in very handy when we are dealing with a new and non-standard algorithm and we also want to capture the stepwise math and logic related to the algorithm.

3. Raw cells: These are the simplest of the cells and they display the text written in them as is. These can be used to add text that you don't want to be converted by the conversion mechanism of the notebooks.

CHAPTER 7

Neural Networks and Deep Learning

Deep learning has become one of the most well-known representations of Machine Learning in the recent years. Deep Learning applications have achieved remarkable accuracy and popularity in various fields especially in image and audio related domains. Python is the language of choice when it comes to learning deep networks and complex representations of data. In this section, we briefly discuss ANNs (Artificial Neural Networks) and Deep Learning networks. Then we will move on to the popular Deep Learning frameworks for Python. Since, the mathematics involved behind ANNs is quite advanced we will keep our introduction minimal and focused on the practical aspects of learning a neural network. We recommend you check out some standard literature on the theoretical aspects of Deep Learning and neural networks like Deep Learning by Goodfellow and Bengio, if you are more interested in its internal implementations. The following section gives a brief refresher on neural networks and Deep Learning.

Artificial Neural Networks

Deep learning can be considered as an extension of Artificial Neural Networks (ANNs) . Neural networks were first introduced as a method of learning by Frank Rosenblatt in 1958, although the learning model called perceptron was different from modern day neural networks, we can still regard the perceptron as the first artificial neural network.

Artificial neural networks loosely work on the principle of learning a distributed distribution of data. The underlying assumption is that the generated data is a result of nonlinear combination of a set of latent factors and if we are able to learn this distributed representation then we can make accurate predictions about a new set of unknown data. The simplest neural network will have an input layer, a hidden layer (a result of applying a nonlinear transformation to the input data), and an output layer. The parameters of the ANN model are the weights of each connection that exist in the network and sometimes a bias parameter.

This network is having an input vector of size 3, a hidden layer of size 4, and a binary output layer. The process of learning an ANN will involve the following steps.

1. Define the structure or architecture of the network we want to use. This is critical as if we choose a very extensive network containing a lot of neurons/units then we can overfit our training data and our model won't generalize well.

2. Choose the nonlinear transformation to be applied to each connection. This transformation controls the activeness of each neuron in the network.

3. Decide on a loss function we will use for the output layer. This is applicable in the case when we have a supervised learning problem, i.e. we have an output label associated with each of the input data points.

4. Learning the parameters of the neural network , i.e. determine the values of each connection weight.

We will learn these weights by optimizing our loss function using some optimization algorithm and a method called backpropagation. We will extend these topics when we actually use neural networks.

Deep Neural Networks

Deep neural networks are an extension of normal artificial neural networks. There are two major differences that deep neural networks have, as compared to normal neural networks.

Number of Layers

Normal neural networks are shallow, which means that they will have at max one or two hidden layers. Whereas the major difference in deep neural networks is that they have a lot more hidden layers. And this number is usually very large. For example, the Google brain project used a neural network that had millions of neurons.

Diverse Architectures

we have a wide variety of deep neural network architectures ranging from DNNs, CNNs, RNNs, and LSTMs. Recent research have even given us attention based networks to place special emphasis on specific parts of a deep neural network. Hence with Deep Learning, we have definitely gone past the traditional ANN architecture.

Computation Power

The larger the network and the more layers it has, the more complex the network becomes and training it takes a lot of time and resources. Deep neural networks work best on GPU based architectures and take far less time to train than on traditional CPUs, although recent improvements have vastly decreased training times.

Python Libraries for Deep Learning

Python is a language of choice, across both academia and enterprises, to develop and use normal/deep neural networks. We will learn about two packages—Theano and TensorFlow—which will allow us to build neural network based models on datasets. In addition to these we will learn to use Keras, which is a high level interface to building neural networks easily and has a concise API, capable of running on top of both TensorFlow and

Theano. Besides these, there are some more excellent frameworks For Deep Learning. We also recommend you to check out PyTorch, MXNet, Caffe (recently Caffe2 was released), and Lasagne.

Theano

The first library popularly used for learning neural networks is Theano. Although by itself, Theano is not a traditional Machine Learning or a neural network learning framework, what it provides is a powerful set of constructs that can be used to train both normal Machine Learning models and neural networks. Theano allows us to symbolically define mathematical functions and automatically derive their gradient expression.

This is one of the frequently used steps in learning any Machine Learning model. Using Theano, we can express our learning process with normal symbolic expressions and then Theano can generate optimized functions that carry out those steps.

Training of Machine Learning models is a computationally intensive process. Especially neural networks have steep computational requirements due to both the number of learning steps involved and the non-linearity involved in them. This problem is increased manifold when we decide to learn a deep neural network. One of the important reasons of Theano being important for neural network learning is due to its capability to generate code which executes seamlessly on both CPUs and GPUs. Thus if we specify our Machine Learning models using Theano, we are also able to get the speed advantage offered by modern day GPUs.

In the rest of this section, we see how we can install Theano and learn a very simple neural network using the expressions provided by Theano.